Raspberry Pi 2

The Disaster to Master Step By Step User Guide

By Matt Eleck

Introduction

I want to thank you and congratulate you for downloading the book, *"Raspberry Pi 2: The Disaster to Master Step By Step User Guide."*

You have most likely have heard about the new Raspberry Pi 2. This is the newer model of the Raspberry Pi that was launched a few months ago. It has the same capabilities as the Pi 1 but has much more RAM and a very fast CPU. This new speed and power has changed the possibilities of Raspberry Pi. Developers and programmers are so excited with the wide range of opportunities that can be achieved with this new version.

The Pi 1 revolutionized the way developers worked with embedded systems. It brought about a new way of doing things with a small embedded system. At $35, it enabled many people explore new areas that only the business support world could have previously done. The Pi 2 has not only enhanced these possibilities, but it has brought a new age where developers are able to write complex control systems using languages and operating systems only used before in the business world. The Pi 2 goes for the same cost as well.

Having said all that, Raspberry is not just a tool for the geeks; even the average computer user will find it very helpful. In the home and school setting, the Pi 2 will come in handy in your projects, as a programming tool, or even as a Home Theater PC. In fact, it has taken the electronics world by storm. The ability to use it for gaming, live streaming, playing HD videos, basic desktop functions, and much more is truly exciting.

In this eBook, we are going to go through the process of setting up your Raspberry Pi 2, installing the different operating systems, installing Wi-Fi, troubleshooting, and everything in between. We shall also look at some of the cool things you can do with your Raspberry Pi 2. This eBook is written in a simple language that will suit a beginner to the world of Raspberry.

Thanks again for downloading this book. I hope you enjoy it!

Table of Contents

Chapter 1

Differences between Raspberry Pi 1 and P2

Raspberry Pi 2 is a small computer that is more or less the size of a credit card. You can connect it to a TV or monitor and keyboard to use it as a general-purpose computer. However, it has still found many uses in developer projects due to its low cost and versatility. It comes as an exposed circuit board without any casing. This is pretty much similar to the Pi 1. Let us now focus on the differences.

The Raspberry Pi 2 replaced the Pi 1 models. The Pi 2 has a 900 Megahertz (MHz) quad-core Advanced RISC Machines Cortex Central Processing Unit. It also packs 1 GB of RAM. These are the main hardware differences. The Raspberry Pi 1 had 256 MB of RAM and a 700 MHz quad-core CPU. This represents the first time the company has upgraded the CPU after trying to improve speed and memory through other ways (mostly software). The improvement to the multi-core 900 MHz Broadcom BCM2836 SoC is responsible for the increased speed. The increased memory enables the running of complex operating systems and programs. These upgrades make Pi 2 perform roughly six times better than previous Pi models.

Just like the PI 1, the Pi 2 has the same four USB ports, forty GPIO pins, an Ethernet cable, a micro SD card slot, a

HDMI port, a composite video and 3.5 mm audio jack, CSI, DSI, and a VideoCore 43D graphics core. The 4 USB ports supply up to 1.2A of current. This enables the connection of more components, even those that are power intensive.

The new Raspberry Pi 2 is able to run a wider range of the ARM GNU/Linux distributions, the Microsoft 10 I0T, and the snappy Ubuntu core due to the change in the architecture from the ARMv6 instruction set to the ARMv7 and advancements in the processor speed and memory. We shall be looking at these operating systems in more detail and how to install them.

The Raspberry Pi 2 is fully backwards compatible with the Pi 1 and all the projects, software, and hardware that were used on the Pi 1. It is able to integrate all the projects that were on Pi 1, but it performs at a higher level due to the increased power. This ensures a seamless transition for those willing to upgrade. It has a complete identical form factor to its predecessor, even after managing to pack much higher power. All connectors are in the same place, retaining the same functionality. This means that any case or third party board add-ons you were using before will still fit onto the new Pi 2. The circuit board is still run from the 5V micro power adapter.

One thing that the Raspberry foundation should be commended for is sticking with the same price even with the added power. In fact, they have been responsible for bringing down the prices of embedded computers on the market. Before Pi 1, it was not possible to find them at prices any lower than $100. This has enabled more enthusiastic programmers, hobbyists, and students to try out their different coding skills on an inexpensive platform. Even for gamers who want increased functionality and possibilities in their video games, it has come in handy.

To demonstrate the increased performance of Pi 2 over the previous models, the Raspberry foundation created a quick test using a Python script that calculates the approximation of Pi's speed then displays it in visual form in the popular Minecraft game. The Pi 1 used 47 seconds to complete this calculation, while the Pi 2 used just three seconds. The quad-core processor is that fast. However, the speed will also depend on whether you have optimized your Pi 2 to run multithreaded, which we will be looking at later. No matter how you use Raspberry, you will notice a bump in performance once you upgrade to the Pi 2.

With all the added power and functionality it brings, the Pi 2 is the one thing you should have. The extra flexibility over previous models that allows you to install and run a wider range of operating systems, including Windows 10 IoT operating system for builders and creators, will make it more popular with all it can do.

Chapter 2

Getting the Pi 2 Operational

We shall discuss how to get your Pi 2 operational in this chapter. I will be assuming you are a beginner and thus start from scratch. Advanced Pi users might find some information basic and common sense but one thing I have learnt in electronics is that you should never assume.

Purchase Your Raspberry Pi 2

Of course, the first thing to do is purchase the Raspberry P2. It will go for around $35. However, due to the popular demand at times outstripping the supply, you might find some people selling the Pi 2 at a higher rate. You can also purchase it from the official store of the Raspberry foundation. As we saw earlier in the first chapter, it will not have a case. It does not need one to function, but it is important to acquire a casing for it. This is basically for protection purposes. You have a choice to either purchase one or make one. I suggest that you purchase the casing when purchasing your Pi 2. They don't go for much. With $5, you will get a decent casing that will not only keep your device well protected, but will also be good for aesthetics purposes. If you had any version of the Pi 1, rest easy, because the Pi 2 comes in the exact same form and you can use the same casing. Some stores will offer a package that consists of the Pi 2, casing, and other peripheral equipment that you need. You can also buy an official casing from Raspberry.

Gather Hardware and Peripherals

The second thing you need to do is to gather the hardware needed for your Pi 2. These will not come with it, and you have to source them. If you already have them with you, that is even better. Users of Pi 1 will have most of them. You will need a micro SD card for the operating system. This is where the OS image will be loaded before you plug into the Pi 2. An 8 GB class 4 SD card is recommended. You will also need a 5V Micro USB power source. This is probably the same USB charger you use for your phone; however, we strongly recommend getting a high quality charger that will consistently deliver 5V and at least 700mAh of power. A low quality charger delivering inconsistent power is the leading cause of unstable systems and problems on the Raspberry Pi. Using a slightly higher rated charger will not harm your Pi. You will need a desktop monitor or a TV to act as a display and a USB keyboard for typing in your commands, though this will depend on how you plan to use your Pi 2. A USB mouse will come in handy. A USB Wi-Fi adapter is essential if you plan to use wireless Internet, though the Pi 2 has an Ethernet port for wired connections. A USB Bluetooth adapter will also be useful in hooking your Pi 2 with other equipment. It is not absolutely necessary to have the Wi-Fi and Bluetooth adapters, but they will greatly help when you need to move your Pi 2 to your project location, for example, rather than bringing your project in to where the Pi 2 is located.

Choosing and Loading Your Operating System

The third step is to load the operating system. With Pi 2, there is the option of loading many different operating systems. I will dedicate a whole chapter for this and how to load the different operating systems. However, the basic principle is that you will be loading the OS onto an SD card using another computer. You will need to download the OS image. The best OS for a beginner is the Raspbian operating system. It is easy to use and will introduce you quite well to the Linux world. Once you understand this OS, you will be in a position to use all other operating systems without any trouble. This is the default operating system and is found on the Raspbian website. I will be talking all about operating systems in the next chapter.

Plugging In Your Raspberry P1

When you have all the needed hardware and the operating system, it is now time to plug in.

You will begin by slotting in the SD card slot. It only fits one way, and thus you will realize if you are putting it in the right way.

Then, plug in the USB mouse and keyboard in the USB slots provided. Also connect the monitor or TV using the right cable and select the right input. Most devices will use the HDMI input. Make sure that it is turned on.

You can plug in the Ethernet cable if you wish to connect your Raspberry to the Internet. You can skip this step for now, but you will need to update firmware at some point.

The last step is to plug in the power supply. This action turns on and boots up your Pi 2.

If you did something wrong, your Raspberry will not boot, and you will need to check and start all over again. This will mostly have to do with loading the operating system on the SD card. When it boots correctly, a setting screen will appear that will prompt for a login.

The default login details for Raspbian is the username *pi* and the password *raspberry*. When typing the password, you will not be able to see any writing; just type the password and hit enter. You will be able to change the username and password to your liking. This is highly recommended, as you might be handling a sensitive project with which you will not want anyone meddling. This is the same reason we have passwords for our PCs.

After you successfully log in, you will see a command line *pi@raspberrypi~$* to load the Graphical User Interface. You will need to type *startx* then press enter.

Your Pi 2 is ready for use, and you can start installing the programs you need.

Chapter 3

Installing OS onto your Pi

Unlike the traditional computer, the Pi does not have BIOS. This is a drive that supports removable media, which helps in OS installation. Other computers will have a DVD drive and a hard disk inside, making it easy to install OS using a disk drive. However, on PI, you will go about it differently. It only has a small solid state drive. This means that you have to install the OS using an SD card prepared on another computer. This will be the only time your Raspberry Pi will depend on another computer. After this stage, it gains full rights to be called a computer by itself.

Some SD cards today come pre-installed with the Raspbian OS, so you just need to plug and power up your Pi. However, if it does not, you need to download the OS image file and store it on your SD card. You might also be interested in learning this process to be able to change your OS any time you need to do so. This is part of the versatility of the Pi 2; you will be capable of running many operating systems depending on the task at hand, since it is very easy to install one.

In this chapter, I will presume that we are using the Raspbian OS, which is the default operating system for the Raspberry Pi. It is worth noting that this is the best for beginners, but there are other options that you can explore later. I will dedicate a whole chapter to comparing different operating systems and instructions on how to install them. All other operating systems, bar the Windows 10 IoT Core, will follow this same process of installing.

To start, have your SD card ready, and make sure it is a high quality one – preferably 8 GB and above class 4. They do currently come cheap. Go to the Raspberry Pi foundation website and get a copy of the Raspbian Wheezy. Wait for the download to finish on your computer before transferring it to your SD card. You will need to copy this file as an image to your card.

If you are using a Windows operating system, many software programs will enable you to copy this file as an image. In the Linux and OS X system, you can use the DD command if you are comfortable with it. In Windows, one of the programs to use is Win32 Disk Imager. It is very straightforward. You will need to install it and then extract the .IMG file from your Raspbian .Zip file. When you are sure of the location to where you have extracted this file, run the Win32 Disk Imager. From within the program, select the image file you just extracted and the drive letter of your SD card where you want to copy it. Write the disc and finish; it is that simple. Note carefully that you need to note the drive letter of your SD card. Not doing so and choosing another drive on your computer will lead to formatting of that drive and loss of all data that was present. Double check if you have to.

Flushing from Linux

1. Open a terminal from your distribution's applications menu.

2. Plug your blank SD card into a card reader connected to the PC.

3. Type sudofdisk -l to see a list of disks. Find the SD card by its size, and note the device address (/dev/sdX, where X is a letter identifying the storage device. Some systems with integrated SD card readers may use the alternative format/dev/mmcblkX — if this is the case, remember to change the target in the following instructions accordingly).

4. Use cd to change to the directory with the .img file you extracted from the Zip archive.

5. Type sudodd if=imagefilename.img of=/dev/sdXbs=2M to write the file imagefilename.img to the SD card connected to the device address from step 3. Replace imagefilename.img with the actual name of the file extracted from the

Zip archive. This step takes a while, so be patient! During flashing, nothing will be shown on the screen until the process is fully complete.

After this step, you should eject the SD card and plug it into your Pi 2. After confirming everything is in order and all cables are connected properly, boot up your Pi by plugging in the USB power cable. Note that the Raspberry Pi does not have a power button, and once you plug in the USB power cable, it starts booting. Make sure you only do this as the last step.

You will see a boot sequence if you have a monitor or TV attached. It will scroll rapidly before your Pi 2 kicks into the Raspi-config utility

At this stage, we can complete some basic configuration tasks that will enhance the functionality of our Raspberry Pi. However, it is not mandatory to do these tasks at this stage, as you can always run the Raspi-config tool at any time.

Just as the Raspi-config tool will show, I will quickly take you through each of these stages and the task you should do at each stage to configure and customize your RasPi.

Expand_rootfs

You should run expand_rootfs. This expands the root partition to fill the entire SD card. By default, the Raspbian will only use as much space on your SD card as the operating system requires. The other space will be left unused. To expand the storage space and make use of the entire SD card, you need to run this task. Any future projects will require this space, and that is why we insist on a higher capacity SD card to have a good amount of storage for future use. You will use the arrow keys on your keyboard to get down to expand_rootfs, then hit enter. You will get some text that will scroll past, and then this message will appear: "Boot partition has been resized. The file system will be enlarged upon next reboot." Hit enter to say OK.

Overscan

Overscan basically means enabling the Pi to use a maximum amount of space on your screen. Not every user will require this; only those who notice that there are significant amounts of blank space around the edges of their screens. Arrow down to overscan, then select the enable option.

Configure_keyboard

This command will be used to configure non-US keyboards and enable their character layouts.

Change_pass

This allows you to change the default password to whatever you wish.

Change_locale

This is necessary for non-English speakers. It enables locales in the operating system.

Change_timezone

Set this depending on your geographical location to enable your RasPi to keep accurate time. When you do this, a script will run at the bottom of the screen before returning you to the main window.

Memory-split

This alters how the system allocates shared memory between the GPU and the main processor. Leave this for the time being, but if you have used RasPi before, you can tweak it to your liking.

Overclock

This means increasing the processor speed beyond what the manufacturer has set. The Pi 2 currently has a 900 MHz processor; you can clock it to 1000 MHz without any problem. On most devices, you void your warranty once you do this, but for the Pi, you do not. In fact, the Raspbian foundation encourages this if you have a project that needs a higher processor speed. For a beginner, leave this for after you get used to your Pi.

Ssh

This enables you connect to your RasPi over a network, so it is very important. Enable this server by turning it on.

Boot_behaviour

At this stage, we choose whether we want the Raspberry Pi to boot to the command line or the desktop environment. By default, it will boot up to the command line – change this to the desktop. When you select boot_behaviour, a question asking "Should we boot straight to the desktop?" pops up. Hit enter to indicate yes.

The last stage is the update. This is not necessary since you just downloaded the OS image. However, any other time you run the Raspi-configtool, you should update. If you purchase the SD card pre-installed with the OS image, you should run the update to get the most recent version, as well a list of updated programs.

Arrow down and select finish. Your RasPi will prompt you to reboot, which you should. Then, take a few minutes to relax as the boot sequence scrolls by. When it finishes, it will take you straight to the Raspbian desktop. Here you will need to do a few more configuration tasks to get you ready, including configuring your network connectivity, which brings us to our next chapter.

Chapter 4

Configuring Network Connectivity

Connection to the Internet is something that you will most definitely need with your Raspberry Pi 2. You can connect either via an Ethernet cable or by using a Wi-Fi adapter. In this chapter, we are going to look at how to go about it.

Connecting via Ethernet Cable

This is pretty straightforward. It is as simple as taking an Ethernet cable, connecting it to the back of your router, and to the Ethernet port on your RasPi. When you plug in the cable, you should see the network LEDs flicker

Since you are most probably using a home network, you should be able to connect to it directly without any other configuration. However, your router needs to be connected to the Dynamic Host Configuration Protocol (DHCP). This service runs on the home network and issues unique IP addresses to any devices connected to the router through Wi-Fi or Ethernet cable. If you find your RasPi not connecting to the Internet, check for DHCP and turn it on. You have to access the router through another computer that is connected to the router.

Connecting via Wi-Fi

Depending on how you bought your Raspberry Pi 2, you may have a Wi-Fi adapter, or you probably have one lying around in your home. Most beginners will look for the whole package when buying so that they have the Pi 2 and all the peripherals included in the package. Advanced users or geeks will just need the circuit board, as they will most probably have these peripherals lying around somewhere. Most Wi-Fi adapters, even the low cost ones, will work just fine. What you need to take care of at this point is to make sure your USB charger is working, since Wi-Fi tends to use up substantial amounts of power. Some Wi-Fi adapters will even have their own power.

The RasPi 2 will have a Wi-Fi config icon on the desktop. Double-click on it and click the scan button to search for available networks.

Enter your password in the PSK slot and click add at the bottom of the window. This action will return you to the scan page. Close it and go back to the wpa_gui. This should show that the RasPi has connected to the network. You should also be able to see your IP address on this window. This is where you will obtain the IP address in case you need to input it somewhere. If you plan to use your RasPi without a screen, write the IP down for future reference. If you do not find your Wi-Fi network, go back to your router using another computer and confirm that the router is broadcasting SSID. Open your router and navigate to the SSID setting and turn it on.

You need to test if the network is actually working and if you can access the Internet. You can do so by clicking on the Midori browser on the desktop. Type in any website you would like to visit; for example, choose one that you visit regularly. When it opens, you can be sure of your hard work and start enjoying the advantages of your small supercomputer. In fact, browsing on your RasPi will be one of your favorite things to do, as it is super-fast. Midori is a lightweight browser that works just as well as other browsers.

After making sure your RasPi can access the Internet, close the Midori browser and go to the last stage. I know you are excited by the functionality, but we need to finish this so that you can use your RasPi fully without any problems.

The last stage is updating the software. It's very important to run a basic software update before you start using your RasPi. This is not an operating system update but a system-wide update, including that of the firmware.

You should type in the following command on the LXTerminal:

sudo apt-get update && sudo apt-get upgrade

This command instructs Raspbian to search for system updates and upgrades. If any such update or upgrade is discovered, a prompt to approve or disapprove the changes will be displayed. You should confirm using the Y key.

You will need to be patient at this stage, since this will take a few minutes and may even appear to hang, especially when using Wi-Fi. It will have to unpack and install the updates. When it finishes, reboot your device for the changes to take place.

At this stage, I am happy to inform you that you have installed the operating system, configured a network to access the Internet, and updated your system, so you are good to go. You can start using your Raspberry Pi 2 as you wish.

In the remaining chapters of the book, I will be talking about adding further functionality, installing different programs, the different operating systems you can explore after you get a grasp on Raspbian, troubleshooting, and anything else that comes up.

Chapter 5

Operating Systems You Can Install On Your Raspberry Pi 2

One of the greatest advantages of Raspberry is the fact that it helps newbies learn programming in a safe environment. In fact, originally, the Raspberry foundation intended to come up with a low-cost minicomputer that would enable students to learn computer science. The low cost was key, since price is one of the prohibiting factors for students and beginners. The Raspberry Pi comes in a very basic form (just a circuit board) and with the conscious decision to keep the costs low. All additional peripherals are assembled as needed, and in many cases, they can be found lying around at school, home, or work. The Raspberry Pi project has been very successful, as it went beyond the expectations of the manufacturers to the extent of running out of stores at one point. Its wide usage in not only schools for projects and programming but also in offices and homes for playing games, HD videos, everyday computer applications, and more has been the responsible for this success.

To enable users to learn programing and the different languages, the Raspberry Pi 2 supports a wide range of operating systems. Most of these operating systems are developed using Linux due to its unique versatility. Most beginners will install the Raspbian OS, as it is the default and most widely used. I would advise anyone to install it first and learn more about it before venturing into other operating systems. It is also widely supported, with over 30000 programs. However, there are other operating systems that will work better for specific projects or functionality.

There are some considerations that will drive a Raspberry user to choosing one application over another besides functionality.

Package Manager - Since most operating systems are based on Linux, most users will look to check the package management tools and package format to form a decision regarding which Linux distribution system to use. Package Manager in the Linux world is the tool that enables users to connect to repositories to download applications. This concept of package repositories is what makes Linux quite popular with many programmers and developers. Even if you are a beginner, this will be a great opportunity to connect with the programmer's world and have access to all manner of applications. The leading package tools are based on the Debian repository, hence the popularity of Raspbian OS.

Multimedia - This is another key consideration, as some operating systems are highly optimized for this. Many people are using the RasPi as a multimedia center, hence this consideration. We shall be looking at which operating systems favor this type of user. The downside to this is that when you take this route, you will not be able to do some other things.

Desktop - The desktop environment is another key consideration when choosing an OS. The screen layout, desktop applications, and menus offered in the different systems will heavily influence users. Some systems even leave out the desktop completely and boot to the command line, where you can then navigate to what you want.

These systems will also be similar in very many ways. They will offer same applications, and some will even share repositories. Let us look at some of these operating systems and what you can achieve with each.

Raspbian Operating System

Raspbian OS is the default operating system for the Raspberry Pi. It does not come pre-installed; you have to do this yourself. You download the OS image from the official website and load it onto an SD card; we covered this in an earlier chapter.

The good thing with this OS is that it has been optimized for the Raspberry Pi hardware and can access over 35000 Raspbian packages. This OS is continually being developed to make it more stable, making it the best starting point for a beginner. It descends from the Debian system. It closely resembles Windows, making it very easy to navigate even for first time Linux users. Upon booting, it starts the config_tool, which enables customization of key settings. In fact, this is the best system to get for learning Linux. Once you understand it, you will have no trouble using other Linux-based distribution systems.

Raspbian OS comes in two formats: the soft float and the hard float. The difference between these two is in how they handle the floating-point numbers. The hard float is the most commonly used since it is faster. The soft float is normally used if you want to program in Java or run applications written in Java.

For users who want to consider Raspberry Pi 2 as their general computer, this OS will be the best for them alongside beginners and students who have not gotten into the depth of programming. It will have or support basic computing programs such as word processors, multimedia, graphics, and a very light and super-fast browser, and you can add much more depending on your preferences. The support from the ever growing Raspbian community and the continuous development makes this OS very appreciated even among advanced Pi users.

Open Source Media Center (OSMC) Operating System

OSMC is the successor to the Raspbmc operating system. This was formerly the media center OS for Raspberry Pi 1 models. With the Pi 2, OSMC is the new name of the operating system. Just as the name suggests, it enables the user to use the minicomputer as a media center. You can watch HD videos stored locally or online, play music, watch TV, work with a remote control such as your phone, watch photos, and play videos from premium services including Amazon, Netflix, and Hulu using the Playon Media server.

For those users who want the complete experience when it comes to multimedia usage, including gaming, you should try out this OS. It is still being developed to increase support and functionality for other uses, but it is currently the best OS to use as a multimedia center.

Just like many other operating systems, installing it is very easy. You will need to download it and save it as an image on your SD card. You should then follow the instructions until it installs. For your SD card, you should find a high capacity card, since you will most likely be using it as a storage space for your media items and we know they can use up considerable space.

Navigating the menu of this OS is easy and straightforward. There are many add-ons available for this OS to support the ability to function as a media center depending on preferences among users.

RISC Operating System

The RISC operating system was developed by Acorn Computers and designed to run on the ARM chipset. It is a fast, compact, and efficient OS. What makes it different from all other operating systems is that it is not a version of Linux or Windows. It was developed independently by the ARM team.

RISC OS for Pi supports a small set of utilities and applications. It has a browser known as NetSurf, a text editor, a scientific calculator, and two package managers. You will have to use either of these two to check for programs and software to run on your Pi 2 because RISC OS, being an old operating system, may run into many programs that will not be compatible with the ARMv6 in Pi 2. RISC OS is a good match for RasPi due to being compact, simple, and efficient. It boots quickly, is very stable, and has a lean core. There will be a few differences in how it operates from other usual operating systems. Here, you will make use of the drag and drop feature to open up files. Select a file and drop it into the icon of the appropriate program for it open.

This OS is worth a try, but it is not the best since it seems out of date in today's world. The functionality and support for this OS is not on par with the other operating systems.

Snappy Ubuntu Core

The Ubuntu operating system is fully supported on the Pi 2. With its increased RAM and processor speed, the Ubuntu OS has come in handy. Ubuntu is very popular among Linux users. Snappy Ubuntu core is a new OS version that fits into the Raspberry Pi 2 quite nicely. It came about as a result of the collaboration between the Raspberry Pi foundation, The Canonical, Ltd., and the Ubuntu community. It was aimed at getting a powerful OS for connecting devices, automation, and robots.

The good thing about this OS is that it gives users total power to customize their system to their liking. This is very useful in the automation and robots areas since each project is unique. The Snappy Ubuntu Core is able to provide updates and reliable construction.

This OS is suited to those who have a project that needs automation. Robots, smart devices, space missions, self-driving cars, drones, smart display systems, and cloud computing projects will be easier when using this OS. In fact, many developers from these sophisticated areas have jumped onto the Pi bandwagon. It is also one of the most secure operating systems when making connection to the cloud.

With the vast knowledge from Ubuntu community, this OS is one to try out, especially if your project is in the aforementioned areas of automation.

Ubuntu Mate

You might be surprised that I have mentioned Ubuntu again. This is yet another Ubuntu Operating System recently developed for the Raspberry Pi 2. It is not in the same league as the Snappy Ubuntu Core, but it is still a good OS, especially when used as a desktop choice. Ubuntu Mate has an active community that has worked very hard over a short period of time to present this OS. A strength this OS has is the vast improvement in the high definition area for video.

Ubuntu Mate would be a good choice for Pi 2 users who want a versatile desktop OS that is capable of varied functions. It is somewhat similar to the Raspbian OS. If you want to experiment with a different OS, you should try this.

The Ubuntu Mate system has some useful applications such as the Mozilla Firefox web browser, the LibreOffice suite, the Mozilla Thunderbird email client, the Shotwell Image Viewer, the Pidgin multi-protocol instant messenger, transmission torrent downloader, and the Rhythmbox audio player.

Open ELEC OS

If you want your Raspberry Pi 2 to serve as a media center, you have two options: the OSMC or Open ELEC (Open Embedded Entertainment Center). Open ELEC is what was formerly known as KODI or XBMC for previous models of Pi. It is a decent operating system for users who want their Pi 2 to serve as a media center, and is lightweight and streamlined for this function.

Chapter 6

Windows 10 IoT Core for Raspberry Pi 2

Microsoft has released the Windows 10 IoT Core for Raspberry Pi 2. This is an operating system for single-board computers that can be used by builders and creators for embedded projects. This system is more of an application than an operating system, since you will not be able to use it like the Raspbian OS and make Pi 2 a stand-alone computer. This does not have a desktop or command prompt. It is meant for use on devices that make use of the Pi 2 as their brain, so to speak, thus the use of the buzzword Internet of Things.

The Window 10 IoT Core is limited to Microsoft's Universal App Platform. It does not have a GUI stack, but has DirectX, XAM, and HTML. To access your Raspberry Pi 2 after installing this OS, you will have to use a development computer or a remote PowerShell terminal. From here, you can run Windows command, but not directly from your Pi 2. Having said that, the Windows 10 IoT core has been well received by developers and creators because it helps them put their devices out there. The Raspberry Pi 2 comes on the cheap, and this OS is free without any royalties to Microsoft for your projects. It will be very important for programmers, builders, and students who are using the RasPi to experiment with a few things.

Devices running this OS are managed through InTune, which is a cloud service, or system center. You will be able to configure updates remotely for these devices and run security patches. Currently, this OS is not fully developed and has a few limitations such as lacking support for Wi-Fi and Bluetooth, which are integral for devices. However, Microsoft is still working on it, and any update will be communicated. Here is a statement from a spokesperson at Microsoft that nicely sums up what the Windows 10 IoT for Raspberry Pi 2 is all about:

"We're embracing the simple principle of helping Makers and device builders do more by bringing our world-class development tools, the power of the Universal Windows Platform, direct access to hardware capabilities, and the ability to remotely debug, update, and manage the software running on Raspberry Pi 2 devices. This Insider Preview release of Windows 10 IoT Core is our conversation-starter. Our goal is to give Makers the opportunity to play with the software bits early and to listen to the feedback on what's working well and what we can do better. You may notice some missing drivers or rough edges; we look forward to receiving your feedback to help us prioritize our development work. We'll be incorporating the feedback we receive into regular software updates along with additional drivers, bug fixes and new features. Those looking for a commercial-quality release should wait for general availability this summer."

To install and run this OS is not much different from what we discussed with the Raspbian OS. The concept is the same; just a few specific details change since this is a Microsoft product.

You will need the following with you before you start the installation process.

- Raspberry Pi 2 (of course)
- 5V USB power cable
- 10GB SD card, which must be a class 10 or higher
- Ethernet cable
- HDMI cable for display (optional)
- A computer running Windows 10
-

To put the Windows 10 IoT Core image onto the SD card, you must use a computer running Windows 10. You must use a physical machine; a VM will not work since you need access to the SD card reader. Follow these steps to configure your SD card so that it is bootable on the Raspberry Pi 2.

- Download the ISO from the Microsoft download center.
- Save the ISO image in a local folder on your computer.
- Double click on the ISO to mount it as a virtual CD drive to be able to access the contents.
- Install "Windows_10_IoT_Core_RPi2.msi"
- When installation is complete, flash.ffu will be located at "C:\Program Files (x86)\Microsoft IoT\FFU\RaspberryPi2"
- Eject virtual CD and insert the SD card.
- Use IoTCoreImageHelper.exe to flash the SD card. Search for "WindowsIoT" from start menu and select the shortcut "WindowsIoTImageHelper"

- Select the SD card then provide the location of the location of the flash.ffu image, then flash the image to the SD card.
- Safely remove the SD card to avoid corrupting the image.

-

Now you have your OS ready, slot it into your Raspberry Pi 2 and connect the Ethernet and HDMI cable. Finally, connect the power supply to start the booting process. At this stage, you can relax for a few minutes as the Windows IoT Core does some boot configurations. It will display the normal blue color you see when Microsoft OS boots. The device will restart once and when it finishes, you will see the Default App appear if you are using a display. You should be able to see your IP address, which you will use to connect to your device either using PowerShell or another computer that shares a network with the Pi 2.

From your computer, install the free Visual Studio 2015 preview in order to access your Pi 2 and play around with it. You will need to use an Ethernet cable to connect your Pi 2 either to a router that the development computer uses or connect directly to the computer, thus setting up ICS (Internet connection sharing).

Using PowerShell to remotely configure and manage your RasPi is something that you will be doing. PowerShell is a task-based command line shell and scripting language. It is designed specifically for system administration. You will be using both PowerShell and Visual Studio 2015.

To initiate a PowerShell session, you will need to find it on your machine by searching for it in the textbox near the Windows Start Menu. Run as an administrator. The first thing to do here is to set up a password for your device by issuing this command:

net user Administrator [new password]

Start a new session with the new password. You will be using PowerShell to connect remotely and view your device or do anything else.

To deploy application, you will need Visual Studio remote debugger. It normally runs automatically after the Raspberry Pi 2 boots. However, after a long period of inactivity, the remote debugger might time out. In such an instance, restart your device. The Visual Studio remote debugger works well with the Raspberry Pi 2.

Chapter 7

Using the Raspberry Pi 2 Camera

The Raspberry Pi 2 supports a camera and video function. This is in line with the company's mission of enabling people to get their hands on a cheap device that is versatile and can be used on many projects. The camera and video function has opened up many opportunities to use the Raspberry Pi 2 on more projects. For instance, this camera has found popular use in home security applications and wildlife traps.

The Raspberry Pi 2 camera can be used for still photographs and high definition videos. People are using it for time lapse and slow motion videos. You will also have access to a wide range of libraries that you can use to create effects in your videos and photos. This module has a 5 MP camera that supports 1080p30, 720p60, and VGA90 video modes. The camera still is at 2592*1944 pixels resolution.

The camera connects to the CSI port, which is the connector closest to the Ethernet port. It connects through a 15 pin ribbon. The CSI (Camera Serial Interface) is a dedicated port designed for interfacing cameras and is capable of high data rates. It connects directly to the processor. The camera board is very lightweight: just 3 grams and measures 25*20*9mm.

To activate the camera module, you need to:

- Update your Raspbian OS to the latest version. A few drivers and tools need to be installed before the camera can work.
- To get the drivers, run the following command *Sudo apt-get update*. This will update the list of available updates for the OS. Then, you will need to run the following command to update the programs: *Sudo apt-get upgrade*
- The next step is to run the Pi configuration menu by going to the following command: *Sudoraspi-config*
- Go all the way to the bottom where you will find the camera module and enable.
- You will then select finish and reboot.

After updating the software, several programs will be available. *Rapistill* will capture images, *raspivid* will capture videos and *raspiyuv* will take uncompressed YUV format images. You will be using the command line to give instructions to the programs. *Raspistill* allows you to take still photos, and *Raspivid* allows you to take videos

These are just the basic commands. There are many subcommands that let you change different variables. If you write the basic commands, your RasPi will give you a lots of those other subcommands.

The Raspberry Pi 2 will support other cameras supported by Linux, such as most webcams. The camera, being a recent addition to the Raspberry computers, has not been fully exploited yet. We can expect more programs to support the camera function in the near future, as well as cases designed to take care of the camera. However, there are projects that have already taken advantage of this camera feature on the Raspberry Pi. Among the notable projects is one in which a bear mascot stuffed with the Raspberry Pi 2 with a camera and GPS has been launched to the edge of space. It has also been used in wildlife photography where a camera version with infrared instilled is being used. The normal camera has the infrared blocking filter installed to match the response of the human eye.

Chapter 8

Troubleshooting

In this chapter, we are going to look at the most common issues that you will probably encounter with your Raspberry Pi 2. As we all know, electronics do not always behave the way we want them to and this can be very frustrating. The user will cause most of these issues either through tinkering with something or by not taking enough caution when handling their Pi 2. However, the essence of this low-cost minicomputer is to enable you play around with it and try out different things. In the process, you get to learn, discover new things, learn about programming and writing code, come up with a cool invention, or many other things. Do not be afraid to play around with your Raspberry Pi 2. Let us look at some of these issues and how to avoid or solve them.

Corrupt SD Card

By now, you must have discovered that an SD card is essential if you have a RasPi device. You will need to find a high quality SD card that will not be easily corrupted. Most SD cards are designed to be written on many times, unlike older SD cards, so do not pick just any SD card lying around and use it for your Raspberry Pi 2. Go for a high quality SD card with at least 4 GB of storage and class 4 and above. If your SD card becomes corrupted, the OS will not boot. Also, remember that your Raspberry will be using this SD card as primary storage for anything you save, though you can set up other storage areas either through the network or a hard drive connected through one of the USB ports.

One thing to remember is that you should always take great care to avoid removing the SD card while your device is still on. This might lead to loss of data, corrupted files, or even damaging the SD card completely. Remember that your system runs from the card entirely. In addition, shutting down incorrectly by unplugging the power cable might damage the operating system. Switch off the device in the correct way either from the desktop or from the command line.

Power

Since your Raspberry Pi 2 relies on power from a 5V USB charger similar to the one used by many smartphones, it is tempting to just use any charger. The downside of this is that some of these chargers are of low quality and will not provide the required amount of power consistently. Remember that your Raspberry Pi 2 will have several peripherals attached to it and they will all depend on this power. These include the keyboard, mouse, Wi-Fi dongle, and anything else connected to it through USB. Thus, a poor quality charger might lead to your system shutting off abruptly due to low amount of power. It is advisable to use a powered USB hub if you find that you need to connect a lot of peripherals to your RasPi 2.

If you find your minicomputer booting up and shutting down immediately after, this is a sure sign that the received power is not enough to run the processor. You will need to have a solid charger with the required output, 5V, and 2 A of current. Another common mistake people make is connecting a USB cable from another source other than a main power supply. Forget how you charge your phone; it will not work on you Pi2. Always connect to a mains power supply using a mains power adapter.

Cables

If you encounter a problem with the Raspberry Pi 2 which was working previously, you should run a quick test of the cables to rule out the problem being there. Check your cables and how they are terminated on both ends. Make sure you use high quality cables; it is easy to struggle with troubleshooting all day long only to realize a certain cable is not in proper working condition. All the cables, including the HDMI, USB, Ethernet, and any others you might connect should be purchased from a reputable manufacturer.

Another common problem associated with cabling is displacing them when fitting cases. Since the Pi devices do not come with any cases, you will have either to make one yourself or purchase one. In the process of fitting one and subsequently connecting the cables, you might either connect a cable wrongly or they may be seated wrongly. Always confirm that all cables are connected properly before you power up your RasPi. The power cable should be the last to be fitted, as this automatically boots up the device.

Cloning Your Operating System

Every Raspberry user appreciates the importance of the SD card containing the operating system. Without it, you cannot start your device, and all of your programs will be no more. Your projects will be compromised. The best thing is to cloning your OS so that even if your SD card was to become corrupted, you could easily get back up in case of anything. Make an image of the operating system and store it on a hard drive where you can easily access it. If you use Windows, this should be easy: use the Win32DiskImager software. Insert the SD card into your computer and run this program. You will find the image file from the SD card and read it to begin the cloning process, browse to where you want to place this image in your hard drive, then click write to finish the cloning process. While you are at it, you can back up anything else on the SD card to your hard drive.

When you have powered up your Pi 2, the LED light should light up. If it does not, no power is coming through; check your main power source and the charger. It should also never blink. It is hardwired to the 3.3V power supply rail and hence should always be on. If it is blinking, your charger is not delivering the required power.

If the red LED is on but the green LED does not flash, it means that the Raspberry Pi cannot find the OS image on the SD card or you have inserted it incorrectly. Remove your SD card and try inserting again.

Keyboard and Mouse Diagnostics

They keyboard and mouse often causes problems for Pi users. If you check into forums, many users ask for assistance on this. Luckily, this is not a major issue.

If you type something with your keyboard and it appears to repeat certain characters, do not freak out; this is a known issue. For instance, you might be typing the command startx and it then appears as Sttttartxxx. Some characters have been repeated and it won't work. This is caused by the keyboard drawing too much power from the Raspberry Pi or a conflict with the USB circuit on the Pi. When you notice such a problem, check your keyboard for the power rating. It will be given in milliamps (mA). This power rating will indicate how much power the keyboard draws from the Pi's USB port. The Pi has a polyfuse on the USB ports, which protects the Pi from devices that attempt to draw too much power. When the polyfuse trips after such an attempt, the USB port shuts off thereby making the keyboard fail to work. The polyfuse trips at around 150mA. If you keyboard has such a rating or higher, it will surely not work properly with your Raspberry Pi 2, so you should connect it to a powered USB hub. Keyboards with LED display lights will often have such a rating or higher.

The issue of repeating characters might also be caused by a lack of enough power on the Pi itself. Check that the Pi is receiving the required 5V of power. Some keyboard models have been known to be incompatible with the Pi. If your keyboard will not work correctly even when everything else is fine, try another keyboard model. The same issues with the keyboard will be common with the mouse.

Do Not Photograph the Raspberry Pi 2

The Raspberry Pi 2 has a known hardware bug: you cannot photograph it with a camera that has a flash. This bug was discovered by one user who noted that in the presence of a bright light, the device reset. The Raspbian foundation acknowledged this bug and explained that it was caused the sensitivity of the u16 power supply chip. The xenon flashes introduce a photoelectric effect, which results in the emission of electrons, which in turn interfere with the activity of the transistors within the chip. Coming in the wake of the excitement caused by the previous Pi models, people were wont to photograph this device. However, you can still photograph it if you place it somewhere with enough light and disable the flash in your camera.

Conclusion

The Raspberry Pi project was meant to enable many students to get access to a cheap computer where they could learn programming and do other tasks. However, it has taken the world by storm. There are thousands of projects running on Raspberry Pi minicomputers as well as millions of users who have found it useful as anything from a general purpose computer to one doing specialized tasks.

Many computing devices today come locked down so that the end user can only use it for the intended function. They do not give room for users to explore and try something different, potentially developing creativity and new innovations. The Raspberry Pi project aims to remove these barriers so that even children and students who are eager to learn programming and play around with things can do so on a cheap computer that they will not be worried about breaking. Besides buying the Raspberry Pi 2, all other needed peripheral items will normally be found at home. An SD card, USB charger, Wi-Fi adapter, Ethernet cable, and HDMI cable are all likely to be found lying around. What is better is that you do not have to share this minicomputer with other people; it can be just for your own projects. Everyone can get one if they wish.

The Raspberry Pi 2 is a continuation of this line, but with added capabilities and the ability support more functions. It has already been used in some fabulous projects all over the world. Some notable projects include a complete weather station, a supercomputer with many Raspberry Pis, web servers, toys, online game servers, gaming console, wireless access point, time-lapse controller, wall calendar, thermal printer, home security applications, and many other uses. Clearly, you can see the limitless opportunities and versatility that the Raspberry Pi offers.

Thank you again for downloading this book!

I hope this book was able to help you with your Raspberry Pi 2.

Finally, if you enjoyed this book and it was able to help you, please take the time to help me by sharing your thoughts and posting a review on Amazon. It would be greatly appreciated!

Thank you and good luck!

www.ingramcontent.com/pod-product-compliance
Lightning Source LLC
LaVergne TN
LVHW052316060326
832902LV00021B/3928